An opinionated guide to

LONDON
FOOD

Written by
DAVID PAW

Koya (no.54)

INFORMATION IS DEAD.
LONG LIVE OPINION.

Why bother reading this guidebook when you can simply look up London's best restaurants online? Because if you do, you'll get 680 million results intermingled with personalised ads for hair products (mine are for hair replacement).

What you have here is – in food terms – a finely reduced sauce of opinion: a short, to-the-point, tasteful guide on where to eat, scoff, munch, slurp and dine your way around the capital. It's where we'd tell you to go if you came to stay on our couch and hated the food we cooked for you. Some of the places in this book are fancy, others are homely; some are cooking traditional recipes exceptionally well, while others are serving up unusual and even groundbreaking flavour combinations. All of them are seriously … what's the word? … *delicious*. Tuck in.

Martin
Hoxton Mini Press

Above and opposite: Chishuru (no.51)

Polentina (no.27)
Opposite: The Quality Chop House (no.8)

Quo Vadis (no.56)
Opposite: Rita's (no.61)

LONDON: A CITY OF FOOD

London is vast, and the sheer array of places to eat can feel infinite. For me, after almost ten years of writing about the city's restaurants, there are some days when the choice still feels as daunting as it did when I arrived here as a teenager, a copy of *Time Out* in hand.

Our city, it must be said, is quite a wonderful place to eat out. But not for the reasons you might think. While the lion's share of attention is paid to anything shiny, monied and central, the best spots in London are buoyed by a sense of purpose and place, whether it's a time-honoured restaurant run by an owner with a passion for old-school French cuisine or a Vietnamese caff serving dishes that soothe the homesickness of its community.

And while there's no getting around the fact that London is awash with money, ours is a city with outstanding, soulful dining at every level – from indie bakeries with social purpose to groundbreaking restaurants that started as market traders – in spite of these riches, not because of them. If you had the excellent taste to pick up this book, you'll be well aware that Michelin stars are only one indicator of quality, not the be-all and end-all.

London's hospitality landscape is defined by the folk who run it, from the workers who grow our produce and butcher the livestock we eat, to the line cook who made your pasta perfectly al dente and the manager who remembers how you like your martini. The restaurant business is an incredibly demanding one at every level, and for those of us privileged enough to dine out with any regularity, the pandemic taught us that we should show up for our favourite places, or risk losing them.

Honour your reservation, and if you *do* have to cancel, give plenty of notice. Put your phone away (after you've taken a thousand pictures of your dinner). Ask your server if they've had a nice day and thank them. Become a regular at a treasured local restaurant.

And remember to enjoy the small acts of kindness that go into a typical lunch or dinner service. Because behind every busy restaurant is a group of people doing their best every night to craft magic and memories for their customers. And to me, that's what restaurants are all about.

David Paw
London, 2024

David Paw *is a writer and editor based in east London. As well as launching The Infatuation and Resy in London, he has also contributed to publications including* Wallpaper*, Eater, Monocle *and* British Vogue.

BEST FOR...

Casual weeknight dinners

Head to Rita's (no.61) for pasta, steak and creative American plates, paired with outstanding cocktails and natural wine. Or go to Berenjak (no.43) for superb Iranian kebabs and stellar bread and dips.

A romantic tryst

The bar at Noble Rot (no.9) might be even better than the main restaurant, and dropping in for a nightcap is a pro move. Over in Soho, Andrew Edmunds (no.59) has atmosphere to spare – handwritten menus, flickering candlelight – and excellent food to back it up.

Impressing out-of-towners

For something special, look to The Clove Club (no.6) for exceptional creative fine dining or Hunan (no.50) for sophisticated Chinese cooking with a neighbourhood vibe. Or go for broke at The Ritz (no.62) or Endo at the Rotunda (no.53) for grand atmosphere and breathtaking food.

Wine and snacks

London does wine bars very well. Perch at the bar in Cadet (no.68) with a glass of something delicious and a plate of charcuterie. Or chat to the passionate team at 40 Maltby Street (no.41) to find a bottle that's unique.

Brunch

The Mediterranean small plates and cocktails at Morito (no.25) are as breezy as it gets, and if it's nice outside, snag a table on the pavement. Esters (no.65) takes brunch seriously, and its imaginative dishes and drinks are worth queuing for.

Vegetarian and vegan fare

Facing Heaven (no.18) is one of the city's best Chinese restaurants, and just happens to be vegan. Meanwhile, breaking bread at pure veg spot Andu (no.16) always feels joyful.

A celebratory evening

Dorian (no.48) is the sort of place that oozes glamour and finesse – provided you can get a table. Or make your way to the legendary Thai restaurant Singburi (no.33) for life-changing dishes from the specials board.

Cost-of-living-proof dining

Much of London's best dining can be found for under £20. There's kebabs and chicken charsi galore at Afghan Grill (no.14), or go all in at Mangal 1 (no.13). Visit one of London's exceptional bakeries for sublime bakes on a dime at Quince (no.71), Eric's (no.38), Popham's (no.31) or E5 (no.24).

Reminding yourself why you live in London

Chishuru's (no.51) West African menu and drinks offer some of the memorable things you can eat anywhere. Or relax beneath a leafy canopy at Rochelle Canteen (no.32) for comforting British fare that wears its excellence lightly.

CUISINES

1

LUCA

Seasonal Italian cooking in luxe setting

Broadly speaking, there are two kinds of restaurants – those that focus on the food, and those that are created to make you *feel* good. Luca packs both style and substance, one of the few eateries that can boast pitch-perfect cooking and an achingly beautiful aesthetic in the same motion. Every aspect of the experience has been considered, from the lush velvet curtain you push past as you enter to the flawless crystal in which cocktails are served. There's an atmospheric terrace for private dinners and a pretty, faux-Tuscan kitchen for rolling pasta that doubles as a private room. The menu of seasonal Italian fare is prepared with the finest British produce, and you'll never want to leave.

88 St John Street, EC1M 4EH
Nearest station: Farringdon
luca.restaurant

2

MASTER WEI XI'AN

Ground zero for spicy hand-pulled noodles

Regional Chinese food has become a firm favourite in London, and this standout restaurant in Holborn is a big reason why. At Highbury's beloved Xi'an Impression, chef Guirong Wei helped popularise hand-pulled noodles tossed in sesame, black vinegar and chilli oil, plus classic Shaanxi fare like roujiamo (Chinese 'hamburgers') or a dish of gently poached chicken with chilli that makes for an excellent introduction to the cuisine. Here, she's flying solo, in a down-to-earth establishment that's perfect for both a knees-up and a celebratory feast – just be sure to arrive on an empty stomach.

13 Cosmo Place, WC1N 3AP
Nearest stations: Holborn, Russell Square
instagram.com/master.wei.3150

3

OTTO'S

Old-school French fine dining

The best restaurants are often run by an owner with a passion for taking care of their guests, and a singular vision of what it means to be hospitable – best exemplified at this beloved bastion of French fine dining tradition. It's clear that its founder and *maitre d'* believes in an old-school approach – there are no sharing plates here, no 'concept menus' – with guests as beneficiaries. Few restaurants nowadays bother to properly flambé a steak or de-bone a fish, but it's part of the standard tableside theatre at Otto's. Prepare to be wheeled out of lunch, full of multi-course lobster and game extravaganzas (two words: pressed duck) and loaded up on good Burgundy.

182 Gray's Inn Road, WC1X 8EW
Nearest station: Chancery Lane
ottos-restaurant.com

4

PARSONS

Captivating British seafood and wine

There are plenty of seafood eateries strewn across central London, but few are as reliably good as this compact restaurant and wine bar a stone's throw from Seven Dials. Expect quintessentially British seafood dishes (fish pie, smoked eel, fried sprats) prepared with top-tier fish and shellfish landed in British waters, served in a charming dining room with a lived-in vibe that feels a lot more old-world than it actually is. The founders also own The 10 Cases wine bar nearby, so the drinks are excellent, making it just as good for an oysters and fizz situation as it is for a bigger party.

39 Endell Street, WC2H 9BA
Nearest station: Covent Garden
parsonslondon.co.uk

5

ST. JOHN

Legendary nose-to-nail British cooking

Described by countless restaurant folk as their favourite establishment, this nose-to-tail icon has much to live up to – and always delivers. Is it the sharp and friendly service, the pleasingly white-washed walls and chatter of a full dining room? Could it be the perfect plates of British fare that land on tables without ceremony, delivering flavour and satisfaction in spades, always washed down with good claret? Or is it that, after so many years, the restaurant *still* takes the business of treating each and every customer like a treasured guest very seriously? It's a place to take your favourite people. Savour the experience further with a few drinks at the adjacent bar after dinner.

26 St. John Street, EC1M 4AY
Nearest station: Barbican
Other locations: Spitalfields, Marylebone
stjohnrestaurant.com

6

THE CLOVE CLUB

Exquisite dishes in a Grade II-listed Town Hall

Depending on your appetite for tasting menus, dinner at The Clove Club could either be the best meal you'll ever have, or a torturous endurance experience. But there's no denying that this hugely influential fine dining restaurant knocks out plates of food so breathtakingly good that you could conceivably think about them on your deathbed (the fried chicken and langoustine, in particular). Don't have three and a half hours to spare? Lunch offers equally ambitious cooking at a quicker clip and lower price point, with the added bonus that the dining room – a grand, colonnaded affair in Shoreditch – looks even more stunning in the light of day.

Shoreditch Town Hall, 380 Old Street, EC1V 9LT
Nearest stations: Hoxton, Shoreditch High Street
thecloveclub.com

7

SESSIONS ARTS CLUB

London's most beautiful dining room

Have you ever been inside a restaurant so beautiful you wanted to weep? The soaring ceilings, period details and contemporary art lining the walls of Sessions Arts Club – found inside the Grade II-listed Old Sessions House in Clerkenwell – rival the grandest buildings in Europe for majesty, while the atmosphere rivals New York for pure buzz. What could easily be a venue to see and be seen in benefits from plates of food created by a talented kitchen that are as thoughtful and delicious as they are aesthetically pleasing, from simple brown butter asparagus to rabbit rillette with grape mustard. In the warmer months, ask for a table on the hidden terrace for drinks and dessert.

4th Floor, 24 Clerkenwell Green, EC1R 0NA
Nearest station: Farringdon
sessionsartsclub.com

8

THE QUALITY CHOP HOUSE

Proudly traditional meat and fish

The name gives away nothing and everything about this hallowed restaurant, where the Grade-II listed dining room – a former working men's canteen – feels idiosyncratic yet perfect for the serious business of eating and drinking, and the food is often faultless. While known for excellent fish and meat (the beef outstrips London's best steakhouses), don't miss the deliciously creative starters and desserts, with offerings like crispy croquettes of hogget with black pepper mayo, confit potatoes or an unbelievable olive oil ice cream. Their sister wine bar next door is worthy of inclusion in its own right, with a more casual (yet no less careful) food offering and plenty of flickering candlelight.

92–94 Farringdon Road, EC1R 3EA
Nearest station: Farringdon
thequalitychophouse.com

9

NOBLE ROT

Effortlessly stylish destination for wine and bites

The original Noble Rot, on Holborn's unbelievably picturesque Lamb's Conduit Street, sets the standard for wine bars that double as restaurants. The cosy space at the front is perfect for great value lunches and evening trysts, with a menu of oysters, charcuterie, fine cheeses and a few small plates. At the back is a dimly lit, intimate restaurant home to impressive cooking with an unabashedly Francophile lean to the food. The wine list has won every award in the land, but there's plenty by the glass and at every price point, all offered in fancy Zalto stemware.

51 Lamb's Conduit Street, WC1N 3NB
Nearest stations: Holborn, Russell Square
Other locations: Mayfair, Soho
noblerot.co.uk

10

THE EAGLE
FARRINGDON

The original gastropub

This characterful boozer has been serving some of London's finest cooking in casual settings for over 30 years. A smattering of tables – large enough for a small party but cosy enough for a date – dot the room, and the open kitchen thrums along at a high frequency, sending out gutsy fare in full view of the pub. The food's the calling card, but you're equally likely to be jostling for elbow room with a local nursing a Guinness as you are an off-duty chef. The daily-changing menu is scrawled on a chalkboard above the kitchen, and food arrives without ceremony on artfully mismatched crockery. Anything grilled or slow-cooked is always a winner here, but the steak sandwich is an event in itself.

159 Farringdon Road, EC1R 3AL
Nearest station: Farringdon
theeaglefarringdon.co.uk

11

BÁNH MÌ HỘI-AN

London's finest Vietnamese baguette

The question is not whether this tiny Hackney lunchtime spot sells the best Vietnamese baguette in the city (answer: unquestionably), but rather, is this bánh mì the best sandwich in London? The crunch and integrity of the rice baguette exposes rivals as pretenders, while fillings are generous, meticulously prepared by the owners and always perfectly balanced. A classic bánh mì (with pâté and charcuterie) or the special (with roast pork belly and soft, folded omelette) are excellent introductions. Ordering the grilled catfish is a badge of honour among regulars.

242 Graham Road, E8 1BP
Nearest station: Hackney Central
Phone: 020 8985 6634

12

BEIGEL BAKE

24-7 Brick Lane institution

London has very few places that could be described as truly for everyone, but this classic Jewish bakery on Brick Lane manages to pull in city workers, students, tourists and east London gentrifiers alike. Most will come for the salt beef beigel, baked moments before, loaded with sliced salt beef and slathered with sinus-clearing English mustard. The rye bread is a better vehicle than the plain bagel for the meat, best eaten either at one of the stainless-steel counters in the shop, or amid the bustle of the street outside.

159 Brick Lane, E1 6SB
Nearest station: Shoreditch High Street
bricklanebeigel.co.uk

13

MANGAL 1

London's quintessential Turkish grill

Mangal 1 is perhaps the most famous of northeast London's Turkish Grills, an old-timer in Dalston that routinely heaves with parties elbow-deep in grilled meat, overspilling baskets of bread, cold beer and ezme salad (to balance out the smoke and protein). Opened by Ali Dirik in 1991 as the city's first ocakbasi (grill) restaurant, Mangal 1 has inspired many others (including the slightly fancier Mangal 2, run by Ali's sons), but the original is still the place to come on a Friday or Saturday night – a boisterous, good-natured affair where the kebabs, grilled over charcoal in the open kitchen for a dose of additional theatre, are as consistent as it gets.

10 Arcola Street, E8 2DN
Nearest station: Dalston Kingsland
instagram.com/mangal_ocakbasi

14

AFGHAN GRILL

The best of the East End kebab houses

This cult Bethnal Green restaurant is a mecca for off-duty chefs and locals in search of succulent grilled meat, kebabs, fluffy naan and copious pours of tea. The staff here are especially sweet and will go out of their way to look after you. If you're stuck, the chopan and chapli kebabs (skewered and tender patties of mincemeat) are both delicious and beautifully spiced. However, real ones know to save space for the flavourful Kabuli pulao studded with tender chunks of lamb or the charsi chicken Karahi, which announces its arrival via a sizzling pan and a hasty round of table Jenga to clear space. Arrive with cash and an empty stomach – you'll need both.

339 Bethnal Green Road, E2 6LG
Nearest station: Bethnal Green
Phone: 020 7613 1444

15

BRAWN

Intimate spot for bold, seasonal cooking

For many diehard hospitality folk, this restaurant on Columbia Road comes close to perfection. The natural wine list is one of the city's best, and staff are unfailingly enthusiastic in offering recommendations. The cooking is a study in balance and flavour, and there's a lightness of touch in the kitchen that makes familiar dishes (Pasta! Pork chops! Panna cotta!) feel like you're experiencing them for the first time all over again. The atmosphere in the whitewashed dining room shifts with the afternoon and evening sun, casting dappled light over wine tasting prints accumulated over decades that cover the walls. The happy din of a dining room in full flow caps off one of London's most pleasurable dining experiences.

49 Columbia Road, E2 7RG
Nearest station: Hoxton
brawn.co

16

ANDU CAFE

Beloved vegan Ethiopian staple

Communal dining is at the heart of Ethiopian cuisine. This Dalston spot is popular for endless reasons, but chief among them is the sheer pleasure of gathering around a platter of injera (sourdough crepe) and loading it with a colourful array of vegetable curries bursting with freshness, flavour and textures. Grip, tear, scoop and eat – then do it again until there's nothing but the shiny steel of the dish in front of you. That Andu is entirely vegan, wallet-friendly and inclusive might come as a delightful surprise; that it's perpetually busy with locals should not.

528 Kingsland Road, E8 4AH
Nearest station: Dalston Junction
anduvegancafe.com

17

ANANTHAPURAM

Electrifying South Indian fare

There are a number of establishments forming a
Keralan constellation within East Ham's galaxy
of South Asian restaurants, but Ananthapuram is
the best, with spot-on Keralan dishes that offer a
glimpse into a distinct and delicious regional cuisine. Gather a few friends to go deep on a menu that
could include plates of crisp, spiced fried chicken
or seafood, whole fish baked in banana leaf, dev-
illed squid or masala crab. Order plenty of rice and
appams to soak up the juices; rinse, and repeat.

241a High Street North, E12 6SJ
Nearest station: East Ham
ananthapurams.com

18

FACING HEAVEN

Vegan Sichuan plates in dive bar setting

One of London's very best Chinese restaurants has neither a Chinese chef in the kitchen, nor a traditional menu. Run by an Angeleno chef, the cooking is a vegan take on classic, fiery Sichuan fare: braised and smoked celeriac slices in fragrant chilli oil, slurpy dan dan noodles or black pepper congee with youtiao (fried dough) cosplaying as biscuits and gravy. The space is pokey, the cramped, neon-lit setup divey, but after several rounds of strong drinks you won't have a care in the world.

1a Bayford Street, E8 3SE
Nearest station: London Fields
facing-heaven.com

19

E. PELLICCI

Classic Britalian caff

Pellicci's couldn't be more of an East End landmark if it tried. Visit this hallowed family-run greasy spoon for a top-tier Full English and you'll end up coming back to catch up with the other regulars and staff. The caff's affable owners possess a Thanos-like awareness of every customer who has ever set foot inside, right down to how they like their tea. Fry-ups aside, there's a Britalian streak to the menu with superlative paninis (crunchy), pastas (hearty) and a lasagne (sultry) that at least one friend swears would be their death row meal.

332 Bethnal Green Road, E2 0AG
Nearest station: Bethnal Green
instagram.com/pelliccicafe

20

BISTROTHEQUE

East London institution for unforgettable brunches

This east London icon has been going for 20 years and counting, long before the area became synonymous with artisanal bakeries and hour-long queues for falafel. Its strengths have remained the same – laid-back bistro plates, great cocktails and unparalleled people-watching in stunning settings – while standards haven't slipped an inch. Brunch is an institution here (arguably the best in London), while the restaurant's drag and cabaret dinners are the stuff of legend. Ascending the pink neon-lit stairway and emerging into a whitewashed, converted warehouse dining room will elicit a gasp from first timers and regulars alike.

23–27 Wadeson Street, E2 9DR
Nearest station: Cambridge Heath
bistrotheque.com

21

ETLES

Big-hearted Uyghur cooking

The Uyghur owners of this soulful Walthamstow spot have done little to adapt their traditional recipes, and their cooking is all the more thrilling for it. Their home province Xinjiang's history as a Silk Road thoroughfare gives a clue to the spicy, multicultural cuisine on offer – comforting hand-pulled noodles, grilled lamb skewers sprinkled with chilli and cumin, plump dumplings and samsas (samosas) still warm from the oven. Everything's halal, the vibe is welcoming and the large serving of Big Plate Chicken could feed a rugby team.

235 Hoe Street, E17 9PP
Nearest station: Walthamstow Central
etleswalthamstow.com

22

MAMBOW

Thrilling Malaysian small plates

The popularity of places like Roti King and Sambal Shiok (no.74) has seen London's appreciation for Malaysian cuisine hit new heights, and this tiny Hackney restaurant pushes the envelope even further. Owner-chef Abby Lee's Peranakan background (ethnic Malay and Chinese) shapes the cooking here, and each dish is her own unapologetic version of the food she grew up enjoying – from crunchy lor bak (five-spice pork wrapped in crispy tofu) and the most extravagant prawn toast around, to herbal pork rib soup, fiery salads and sour curries that beg for an extra order of rice. The DIY-chic dining room has a charming neighbourhood vibe, but make no mistake – this is food worth travelling for.

78 Lower Clapton Road, E5 0RN
Nearest station: Clapton
mambow.co.uk

23
POCKETS

Falafel to empty your pockets for

There's one item on the menu at Pockets and it's one of the best things you can eat in London. But just how good can a falafel pocket be? At this Hackney hole-in-the-wall the answer is, well, *incredible* – so much so that lining up at their original London Fields stall for an hour-long wait was easily justified when you were nose deep in pillowy pita, crunchy green falafel, heavenly amba and tahini and crisp confit potato. Now in a new home around the corner, everything is still painstakingly made in-house, the quality is impossible to dispute and prices are reasonable. But even Beyoncé would have to join the queue – we don't make the rules.

367 Mentmore Terrace, E8 3RT
Nearest station: London Fields
instagram.com/pockets_uk

24

E5 BAKEHOUSE

Top-tier bakery with a side of social change

A modern-day Hackney institution (the clue's in the name), this sourdough pioneer has turned out consistently brilliant loaves for the past decade alongside a pace-setting line of flaky pastries and intricate viennoiserie. The queue outside its London Fields flagship at the weekend may be full of enough E5 cliches to make your favourite meme account proud, but snag one of the few tables to tuck into brunch and you'll see why it's worth the hype. At its core, it's a big-hearted operation, with a focus on sustainability that sees them running their own bakery school, milling their own flour and growing produce on their own farm in Suffolk – as well as supporting change-making community initiatives.

396 Mentmore Terrace, E8 3PH
Nearest station: London Fields
Other location: Poplar
e5bakehouse.com

25

MORITO

Bright Mediterranean flavours in east London

Move over meat-and-two-veg brigade: the appeal of sharing a kaleidoscope of small plates loaded with delicious morsels is undeniable, and in London, it was perfected at Morito. There's a casual flair to the cooking here, with punchy flavours that traverse the Med (from the Levant and Spain to Greece and North Africa) and pair beautifully with exemplary cocktails and natural wine. Don't miss the lamb chops, kissed with rosemary and slicked with anchovy butter, while the vegetable dishes are easily among the city's strongest. The Exmouth Market original is intimate, but the industrial cool of its Hackney sibling is a ball.

195 Hackney Road, E2 8JL
Nearest station: Hoxton
Other location: Exmouth Market
moritohackneyroad.co.uk

26

PLANQUE

Classy plonk and elite bistronomy

A 'wine drinkers' clubhouse' may sound a little elitist, but this Hackney bar, bottle shop and restaurant – with one of the best-stocked cellars in town – is a haven for anyone passionate about vino. To its credit, Planque is also welcoming to those looking to up their oenophile credentials in settings that feel as intimate as a well-off friend's sleek dining room (complete with a long communal table and an open kitchen, naturally). The food here offers just as much reason to visit, with one of the city's most exciting chefs sending out dizzyingly creative plates that recall the best of Paris's modern bistros. Guinea fowl pithiviers, lobster tartines and inventive offal dishes will leave even the most jaded palate elated.

322–324 Acton Mews, E8 4EA
Nearest station: Haggerston
planque.co.uk

27

POLENTINA

Regional Italian cooking inside a factory canteen

An Italian restaurant deliberately specialising in rustic, old-timey grandma recipes might raise an eyebrow among foodie types, but how about one on an industrial estate in Bow? Now, imagine that it's in the former canteen of a sustainable clothing manufacturer – you're right, that *is* an assembly line behind the paned glass. Polentina's one-of-a-kind setting already makes it unique, but the cooking lives up to the premise. Chef-owner Sophia Massarella's love of forgotten regional Italian recipes translates to hearty, warming fare that you won't find anywhere else – Abbruzzese crepes in broth, perhaps, or baked rice from Puglia – plus a short list of Italian natural wines that Sophia will reel off to you herself.

1 Bowood House, Empson Street, E3 3LT
Nearest station: Bromley-by-Bow
polentina.com

28

SUSHI SHOW

Affordable sushi with no compromise

Good sushi is hard to find in London – and the kind that won't necessitate living off instant ramen for the rest of the month is even harder to find. Luckily, this excellent sushi-ya specialises in the kind of sushi and sashimi that spotlight quality fish, vinegar, rice and little else, eschewing any pretensions the average haughty Mayfair institution may upsell you on. While it's primarily a takeaway operation, the Shoreditch shop has a small counter and a few tables where you can order à la carte – and though it's worth paying attention to the specials, the scallop and otoro (fatty tuna) are both reliably good mainstays. They're BYO, so come with your best boutique champagne for an attainably lavish lunch.

136 Bethnal Green Road, E2 6DG
Nearest station: Shoreditch High Street
Other location: Angel
sushishowlondon.com

29

CAFÉ CECILIA

Stylish neighbourhood bistro

Tucked away from the crowds of Broadway Market on Regent's Canal, Café Cecilia may be achingly trendy, but this all-day restaurant is also profoundly lovely. The cooking has strong, seasonal Mediterranean overtones grounded in a British sensibility: crisp sage and anchovy fritti hot from the fryer, proper puddings, handmade pastas and a steak frites in creamy pepper sauce that you'll dream about from the moment you leave. It's a favourite with east London's fashion and art set who pile in at the weekend to feast, but breakfast is when it's at its most convivial and generous, the cafe living up to its name as a friendly neighbourhood space.

32 Andrews Road, E8 4FX
Nearest station: Cambridge Heath
cafececilia.com

wine special   9⁰⁰
negroni   10⁵⁰
vermouth & soda   7⁵⁰
white port & tonic   8⁵⁰
campari & soda   7⁸⁰
gin & tonic   8⁵⁰
vodka & tonic   8⁵⁰
lillet   7⁴⁰
——————————————
poire williams   8⁰⁰
vieille prune   8⁰⁰
Calvados   12⁰⁰
prunne des charentes 8²⁵

30

LYLE'S

The definitive modern British restaurant

This iconic Shoreditch restaurant revolutionised modern British cuisine in the not-so-distant past, with ambitious chefs across the nation adopting its kitchen's rigorous approach to seasonality and 'less-is-more' spirit. There's a short tasting menu at dinner, but lunch is more enjoyable, with an à la carte that rewards spontaneity. Come in spring and summer for astonishing vegetables and sea-food – raw scallop with white grapefruit and roe, or rock oysters with fresh peas in vin jaune – while the restaurant's reputation for stellar game cookery shines in autumn. And though their influence on the London food scene is big, eating in the minimal, tiled dining room flooded with natural light is a sunny, laid-back affair.

Tea Building, 56 Shoreditch High Street, E1 6JJ
Nearest station: Shoreditch High Street
lyleslondon.com

31

POPHAMS

London's pastry and pasta dough dynasty

The original Pophams in Islington left Londoners swooning over covetable bakes – impossibly flaky, buttery pastries and Danishes topped with seasonal British fruit – as well as a minimal aesthetic that made something as mundane as grabbing a latte feel like you were the main character in a Nancy Meyers rom-com. The owners upped the ante with their Hackney bakehouse, though, which functions as a sharp neighbourhood space for oat flat whites during the day and a pasta restaurant par excellence come evening. Grab some mates to convene here for perfect, veg-forward small plates and spritzy cocktails, plus pastas (rolled daily in the open kitchen) that you'll be gushing over in the group chat for weeks to come.

197 Richmond Road, E8 3NJ
Nearest station: London Fields
Other locations: Islington, Victoria Park
pophamsbakery.com/pasta

BOTTLE SHOP

32

ROCHELLE CANTEEN

Seasonal British fare in a school's former bike shed

There are few things in London better than pulling up to a table at this widely adored restaurant hidden away in a Shoreditch square. The location – the former bike shed of a school, accessed by buzzer behind a nondescript door – sounds like a novelty, but the cooking has substance and soul. Somehow always serving *exactly* what you want to eat for the time of year, the food here balances heart and generosity with a certain deftness. It draws a creative crowd, who arrive for spritzes and stunning fish and vegetable cookery during fairer months, while winter offers a comfort blanket of perfect braises, sublime roasts and unmissable puddings.

16 Playground Gardens, E2 7FA
Nearest station: Shoreditch High Street
rochellecanteen.com

33

SINGBURI

Family-run Thai with legendary specials

Singburi is deserving of every accolade bestowed upon it and more, with much of the praise aimed at chef Sirichai Kularbwong's world-class cooking and dedication to his craft. Each dish on the daily-changing chalkboard of specials screams to be ordered – from thrice-fried moo krob (pork belly) humming with chillies and basil to fiery curries and stir fries. But truthfully, Singburi's charm is as much about the intangibles that make it unique, from the old-school BYOB, cash-only approach and the beatific presence of the chef's parents at each service to the community of locals and diehards who brave the pen-and-paper booking system for a coveted spot in the dining room. A treasure.

593 High Road Leytonstone, E11 4PA
Nearest station: Leytonstone High Road
instagram.com/singburi_e11

34

EAT VIETNAM

Astonishingly good Vietnamese BBQ

Here's a hot tip: London's best Vietnamese restaurants are no longer on its pho mile in Dalston, but south of the river. This Deptford gem is beloved by locals and families who travel for flawless renditions of dishes like bánh xèo (crispy Vietnamese pancakes), bánh cuốn (delicate rice crepes stuffed with pork and mushrooms) and superb barbecued meats just begging to be dipped in the house sauce. As an all-round experience it's difficult to beat, and a certified happy place for those who have visited. It gets very busy at the evening and weekends, so be sure to book.

234 Evelyn Street, SE8 5BZ
Nearest station: Deptford
eat-vietnam.co.uk

35

IMONE

Homestyle Korean cooking worth travelling for

The best Korean cooking isn't found in central London, but in the cultural enclave of New Malden, a short train ride from Waterloo. It's worth the trip, and this unassuming cafe serves some of the best dishes around, from beautifully light japchae (stir-fried glass noodles), bubbling pots of kimchi stew and short rib soup, to a standout spicy white-fish served whole with fragrant chrysanthemum leaves. It's an auntie-run affair, with no-nonsense *ajummas* at the helm; and for those who took Hangul classes after watching reality show *Single's Inferno*, the day's specials are written in Korean script and plastered around the dining room.

169 High Street, New Malden, KT3 4BH
Nearest station: New Malden
imonelondon.com

36
KAIETEUR KITCHEN

Guyanese cooking for the soul

Before the old Elephant & Castle shopping centre was razed to build luxury flats, the line for Kaieteur Kitchen would form every lunchtime. Now relocated to a new building, Faye Gomes' Guyanese cooking still draws the crowds. Gomes is a local legend, and with good reason: her food is a love letter to the Caribbean, and each dish emerging from the kitchen of this tiny restaurant is imbued with her warmth and soul. It's impossible to order badly from the daily-changing menu, but her pepper pot (a slow-cooked, spiced stew of oxtail and tender beef) with plantain, pumpkin and spinach rice is a masterclass in flavour and comfort.

Castle Square, Elephant Road, SE17 1EU
Nearest station: Elephant & Castle
instagram.com/kaieteurkitchenoriginal

37

BRAVI RAGAZZI

Seriously good local pizzeria

Neapolitan pizza has become London's most popular style, and it's impossible to start a conversation at parties these days without someone piping up about doppio zero flour and the morphology of tinned tomatoes. In Streatham, Bravi Ragazzi's pies hit all the highs – puffy, blistered crust, a base faithfully recreated with San Marzano tomatoes and fior di latte cheese that bubbles irresistibly when the *pizzaiolo* sticks the whole thing in a wood-burning oven. It's the kind of fun, neighbourhood affair where you can pop in spontaneously without breaking the bank and enjoy sitting elbow-to-elbow with local characters: the epitome of a great pizzeria.

2a Sunnyhill Road, SW16 2UH
Nearest station: Streatham
instagram.com/braviragazzipizzeria

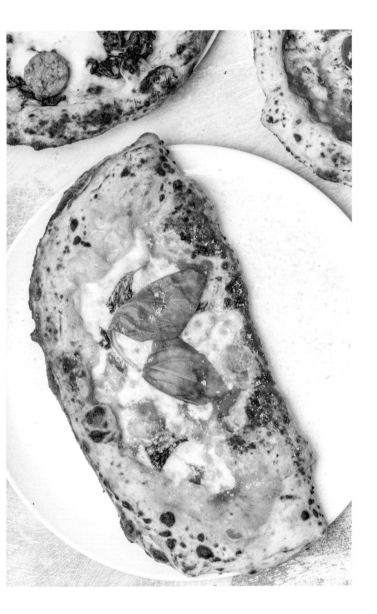

38
ERIC'S

Covetable pastries and specials worth the wait

One of London's finest bakeries, every pastry that this tiny shop and cafe turns out is a marvel of taste and structural architecture, and even casual food lovers will gawp at the intricacy in a simple croissant or pain au chocolat. Seasonal specials keep things interesting (Ferrero Rocher brioche bun, anyone?) and despite it being small, sustainability is still baked into everything – favouring rye and wholewheat flour for extra flavour and to cut down on waste. It's hugely popular, so be prepared to get up early and jostle with half of south London for the last morning bun. But is it worth it? Absolutely.

20 Upland Road, SE22 9EF
Nearest station: East Dulwich
ericslondon.com

39

BAO BOROUGH

Playful Taiwanese fare (with karaoke)

The original BAO was a market stall that begot a hit Soho restaurant, but the popular group of modern Taiwanese restaurants finds its best iteration in Borough. The dining room channels a Taipei night market and the small plates hit hard – if you're experiencing the fried chicken with hot sauce for the first time, we're not-so-secretly jealous. The gua bao (steamed buns) are much imitated but never bettered, though the rice bowls (topped with maitake mushrooms or aged beef and confit egg yolk) are where it's at, washed down with a highball or a Taiwanese beer. The best seats are at the counter where you can watch the chefs do their thing; afterwards, retire downstairs to a private room for karaoke and more cocktails.

13 Stoney Street, SE1 9AD
Nearest station: London Bridge
baolondon.com/restaurant/bao-borough

40

RAMBUTAN

A zesty, lip-smacking trip through Sri Lanka

This Sri Lankan restaurant on the steps of Borough Market is a critics' darling, and with good reason: it blends bold, flavourful cooking with all the features of a zeitgeisty restaurant perfectly. Perch at the long bar with an expertly mixed banana negroni and take in the sights and aromas as chefs toss pots of pristine meat and seafood over open fire – or relax at the back, in a light-filled atrium dotted with tropical plants, while grazing on the signature black pork curry and gundu dosas with spicy green sambol. It's intimate enough for a date, while the sharing format makes it ideal for a small group – but you may also be tempted by a solo lunch at the bar, drink in hand.

10 Stoney Street, SE1 9AD
Nearest station: London Bridge
rambutanlondon.com

41

40 MALTBY ST

Superlative small plates and low-intervention wines

As far as wine bars go, 40 Maltby is pretty much flawless. The railway arch location, intimate atmosphere and crowd of regulars is part of the appeal, while the city's most discerning food writers and chefs make the pilgrimage to eat here, which should tell you everything you need to know about the cooking. Ever wonder how exquisite a simple squash fritter, rillettes or chocolate tart could taste? The answer is pretty damn incredible, and you'll find god-tier versions of humble dishes here. It's walk-ins only, so go early to avoid disappointment.

40 Maltby Street, SE1 3PA
Nearest station: Bermondsey
40maltbystreet.com

42

KAPIHAN

Speciality coffee with outstanding Filipino bakes

From the outside, this tiny coffee shop in Battersea feels like a nice-but-unremarkable addition to the neighbourhood. Peer under the hood, though, and every aspect of Kapihan is a love letter to its owners' native Philippines. Lattes and flat whites eschew the usual espresso in favour of punchy single origin barako coffee, sourced and roasted by the owners themselves; treats include Filipino bibingka (sweet baked rice muffins), cassava cake or a flaky longganisa sausage roll that blends Southeast Asian flavours with British tradition. It's a compelling blend that could only thrive in London, and a perfect expression of everything great about eating in a city that sits at the cross-roads of myriad global cultures.

547 Battersea Park Road, SW11 3BL
Nearest station: Clapham Junction
kapihan.coffee

43

BERENJAK

Modern Iranian grill in the heart of Soho

Stepping from a Soho street into Berenjak feels like stumbling upon a chic hole in the wall in Tehran – albeit one with plush seating and fancy cocktails – but the food is the real deal, thanks to the care lavished upon everything from a plate of pickles to a platter of grilled meat. The menu at this modern Iranian bolthole is simple and it's tempting to over index on breads and dips, but save space for the lamb kebabs, which range from a sublime koobideh to a fillet platter with all the trimmings, designed for sharing.

27 Romilly Street, W1D 5AL
Nearest station: Leicester Square
Other location: Borough
berenjaklondon.com/soho

44

AKUB

A dazzling homage to Palestinian cuisine

Named for the symbolic native plant that's forbidden to forage in the occupied West Bank, this acclaimed Palestinian restaurant offers contemporary riffs on classic dishes: baby eggplants stuffed with fermented herbs, skate kufta in vine leaves or a celebratory dish of chicken Musakhan humming with sumac and onions. Akub owner Fadi Kattan is a leading figure in his nation's foodways, and the kitchen mixes imported Palestinian herbs and spices with British produce. Reminders of the motherland are present throughout the restaurant, in ceramics from Palestinian artists to vintage keys that hang in the dining room and serve as symbols of homes lost under the occupation.

27 Uxbridge Street, w8 7TQ
Nearest station: Notting Hill Gate
akub-restaurant.com

45

CRISP PIZZA W6

Unimprovable pizza in chilled-out pub

The queues at this west London phenomenon may be more Berghain than humble slice shop, but sceptics be warned – the pizza here is very good indeed. These crisp (ahem), foldable, NYC-style slices are pretty perfect: chewy and flavoursome, with toppings that tip their hat to convention and quality (thick-sliced pepperoni, parmesan, burrata, 'nduja). It isn't uncommon to wait an hour for a few slices, but take advantage of Crisp's pub residence: order a few pints, grab a seat wherever you can and soak up the party atmosphere.

25 Crisp Road, w6 9RL
Nearest station: Hammersmith
instagram.com/crisppizzaw6

46
CAFÉ TPT

Homely Cantonese in Chinatown

With regional Chinese fare more popular than ever, it's easy to forget that the backbone of Chinatown was the Cantonese caff, modelled on Hong Kong's back alley *dai pai dongs* (open-air food stalls). TPT is the last of its kind, but still consistently turns out superb renditions of a vast array of dishes, from tender roasted meats to perfectly al dente wonton noodles in workaday surroundings. Beyond the classics, much of the best stuff – baked pork chop rice, curried beef flank – is pure comfort food, with homestyle Cantonese dishes written up and stuck to the walls each day. Go alone, go with a friend, go with a big group – you won't be disappointed.

21 Wardour Street, W1D 6PN
Nearest station: Piccadilly Circus
cafetpt.com

47

BARRAFINA

Seductive Spanish tapas

Is there a more casually glamorous experience in London than pulling up to the bar at Barrafina for a glass of cava and flawless tapas? Years after its original introduction in Soho, this classic Spanish tapas bar remains a special experience, whether it's your first time or your fiftieth. There's the setup – acres of stunning marble, plush leather seating and a long zinc bar to make a design snob weep. Then, of course, everything you eat will be painstakingly sourced, from the freshest seafood caught in British waters to fine cheese and jamon imported from Spain. With everyone sat at a bar overlooking the open kitchen, there's conviviality and theatre, too.

26–27 Dean Street, W1D 3LL
Nearest station: Tottenham Court Road
Other locations: Covent Garden, Borough, King's Cross
barrafina.co.uk/restaurants/dean-street

48

DORIAN

Hot ticket with a star chef

Notting Hill can finally claim to have the hottest restaurant in town, and many a pilgrimage has been made to W11 to pull up at one of the buzziest dining rooms in the capital – even before Dorian was awarded a Michelin star. For its allure, you can blame its star chef's sublime modern bistro cooking with luxurious touches (if you're going to splurge on caviar or fancy wine, do it here). The dining room is glamorous – lit so well that everyone inside it looks like a supermodel – and the polished service belies the restaurant's origins as a hotbed of elite talent. Worth dressing up and going all out for.

105–107 Talbot Road, W11 2AT
Nearest stations: Ladbroke Grove, Westbourne Park
dorianrestaurant.com

49

GYMKHANA

Indian fine dining at its best

Gymkhana represents the pinnacle of Indian fine dining in the capital, with all the trappings of a Mayfair restaurant (The lick of glamour! The gorgeous dining room! The accolades!), backed up by smart service and cooking that lifts staples to giddy heights. Everything on the menu is spectacular, and favourites from the early days – like the kid goat keema and muntjac biryani – have become mainstays for a reason. There's a svelte private dining room for celebratory splurges, as well as a superb bar for cocktails. And though the tasting menu is well worth saving up for, lunch still astonishes at a far more accessible price.

42 Albemarle Street, W1S 4JH
Nearest station: Green Park
gymkhanalondon.com

50

HUNAN

Masterful Chinese tasting menu

Leaving the choice of your dinner in the chef's hands might feel on-trend today, but back when this Chinese restaurant introduced it in the 1980s, it caused quite the stir. Legendary owner Mr Peng hails from Taiwan, and each night his chefs serve an exquisite no-choice tasting menu. The shatteringly crisp tempura green beans and delicate bamboo soup are so good they may just haunt your dreams; if you're with a group, grand supplements like whole spider crab in Shaoxing or lobster noodles are worth it. For serious wine drinkers, the list is one of the city's best, with markups so modest they beggar belief.

51 Pimlico Road, SW1W 8NE
Nearest station: Sloane Square
hunanlondon.com

51

CHISHURU

Game-changing West African food

As feel-good stories go, the rise of this West African restaurant from ambitious Brixton Village residency to Michelin-starred eatery (and the talk of London) is tough to beat. And as dining experiences go, it's utterly unique. Traditional West African dishes like pepper soup and mafe (peanut stew) are given star treatment, and the restaurant has a down-to-earth feel that's reflective of chef-owner Joké Bakare's joyful brand of hospitality. Don't miss the superb cocktails and French-leaning wine list, and while the warm-toned basement dining room is snug, the best tables nuzzle the open kitchen, where you can watch Bakare and her team strut their stuff.

3 Great Titchfield Street, W1W 8AX
Nearest station: Oxford Circus
chishuru.com

52

DARJEELING EXPRESS

Regal Mughlai feasts from an all-women kitchen

It's hard to go wrong at Darjeeling Express, chef Asma Khan's paean to the cooking of her Mughlai heritage. Her dinner menus have become the stuff of legend: an array of curries carried ceremoniously to your table, flanked by breads, pickles and side dishes of homestyle potatoes sautéed with cumin or moreish beetroot raita with spiced yoghurt. Lunch is a more relaxed affair, with an à la carte menu that adds flourishes like plump momos and snacky dishes like chilli cheese toasties. Dinner here feels like an escape thanks to the sleek, modern interior, but the irrepressible buzz of its central London location is always present.

2.4 Kingly Court, Carnaby Street, W1B 5PW
Nearest station: Oxford Circus
darjeeling-express.com

53

ENDO AT
THE ROTUNDA

The ultimate sushi experience

Sushi *omakase* (meaning, 'I leave it to you') restaurants are a fun way to dine, with the focus solely on the food and the interaction with the chefs. It's also expensive, and few are more prestigious than this Michelin-starred big hitter, nestled at the top of the former TV centre in Shepherd's Bush. The space itself (designed by star architect Kengo Kuma) is jaw-dropping: a suitable setting for a meal here. While it may be £250 for 20 small courses, reframe that as 15 of the best mouthfuls you'll ever eat (without the plane fare to Tokyo), and it's a comparative bargain. Just.

8th Floor, The Helios, Television Centre,
101 Wood Lane, W12 7FR
Nearest stations: Wood Lane, White City
endoatrotunda.com

54

KOYA

Japanese small plates and udon

London has by and large been a desert for the kind of focused Japanese cooking that makes the country legendary for its dining culture. Koya is an exception, serving painstakingly made udon noodles alongside a variety of broths, toppings and dipping sauces. Long-time regulars know that the small plates and specials board are where it's at, with apple cider-braised pork belly and mustard being one of the restaurant's classic dishes for a reason. Sitting at the busy countertop and watching the chefs at work while slurping your noodles is a great way to spend an evening – but be warned that it's no reservations, so expect a wait at peak times.

50 Frith Street, W1D 4SQ
Nearest station: Tottenham Court Road
Other locations: Bank, London Fields
koya.co.uk/restaurant/soho

55

THE PALOMAR

Middle Eastern dinner party (emphasis on party)

Tel Aviv's nightlife is noted, and The Palomar is the closest thing you'll get to the party vibe that city is known for. The neon-soaked room and long bar give an indication as to what you're in for. Pull up a stool and perch at the counter to drink shots with the chefs and bartenders in between eating wonderful Middle Eastern small plates (kubaneh bread swiped through creamy labneh, grilled melt-in-the-mouth octopus, succulent lamb chops). Dinner here is one of London's most intoxicatingly pleasurable experiences.

34 Rupert Street, W1D 6DN
Nearest station: Piccadilly Circus
thepalomar.co.uk

56

QUO VADIS

Jeremy Lee's ode to seasonal British food

There is no lovelier place to be spoiled rotten than at this Soho classic, ensconced between pressed linens and lipstick-red leather banquettes, martini in hand and with nary a care in the world. Chef Jeremy Lee's jovial personality illuminates the entire experience, where gorgeous, seasonal British cooking spans hearty pies and roasts to luxurious game, fish, fancy desserts and puddings. Even the menus are stunning to behold, but glance up and you'll notice that the other guests are just as blissfully happy. The staff here have a way of putting you at ease, turning this busy central spot into a friend's dining room. It's about as special as it sounds – which is very.

26–29 Dean Street, W1D 3LL
Nearest station: Tottenham Court Road
quovadissoho.co.uk

57

MOUNTAIN

Spectacular open-fire Spanish cooking

Want to get someone's attention? Take them to
Mountain. This chef-driven restaurant is a jewel
in London's crown, and every aspect of it is a flex,
from the capacious split-level dining room (bright
and buzzy upstairs; cosy and intimate downstairs),
to an open kitchen where chefs cook over flames
and even an on-site bakery. It earned a Michelin star
for its Spanish-inspired take on live-fire cookery
(also a signature at Brat, its famous sister restaurant
in Shoreditch). You'll eat dishes that appear simple
but are breathtakingly delicious, from spicy pork
sobrassada and fresh cheese with anchovies to a
showstopping lobster caldereta to share with a few
friends.

16–18 Beak Street, W1F 9RD
Nearest station: Piccadilly Circus
mountainbeakstreet.com

58
THE HARWOOD ARMS

Michelin-star pub fare in sumptuous surrounds

Pub dining reaches its peak with the Michelin-starred Harwood Arms which, in true Fulham form, is the kind of place you're more likely to see Don Draper than Phil Mitchell. There's wood panelling, svelte leather seating and mounted animal heads galore – but if you're harbouring any faux-proletariat pretensions, these will evaporate when the first dishes hit the table. The Harwood shares ownership, talent and produce with the three-star Ledbury, meaning that the cooking here is rarely less than fantastic, with dishes like Berkshire deer chop, rabbit lasagne and apple parfait giving serious fine dining energy. The Sunday roast is epic, and the venison scotch egg is (predictably) one of the best in London.

Walham Grove, sw6 1QP
Nearest station: Fulham Broadway
harwoodarms.com

59

ANDREW EDMUNDS

Romantic bastion of bohemian Soho

Little has changed at Andrew Edmunds since it opened in 1985. One of the last corners of 'old' Soho, it's the kind of timelessly elegant place to keep in your back pocket for intimate celebrations with nearest and dearest, when you want to feel special but might not want to shout about it. The modern British cooking? Consistently delightful. The wine list? One of the loveliest in Soho. The welcome and warmth from the regulars who became lifers after their first visit? Priceless. In the evening, there's candlelight and every menu is handwritten in cursive script each day. It's that kind of place.

46 Lexington Street, W1F 0LP
Nearest stations: Piccadilly Circus, Oxford Circus
andrewedmunds.com

60

PAUL ROTHE & SON

Legendary sandwich shop and icon of old London

'HOT SOUP' reads the sign on this gleaming white shop facade on a quiet side street in Marylebone. Inside, you'll find a quaint shop-deli, its walls pleasingly stacked with rows of sauces and condiments, a busy counter on one side. Named for the current owner's grandfather, this iconic sandwich shop has stood here since 1900 and is run by the same family – a thriving bastion of old London, if ever there was one. Come here for classics made with respect, to eat in or take away, like coronation chicken on soft white bread or eggs and anchovy. Or go rogue and dream up your own creation; if they have the ingredients, you can order it.

35 Marylebone Lane, W1U 2NN
Nearest station: Bond Street
instagram.com/paulrotheandson

61

RITA'S

Playful modern American dining

There are restaurants you go to for 'proper' cooking, and there are places you go to soak up the buzz. Rita's is the rare kind that excels at both. Loosely modern American in influence, this lively spot started as a series of playful residencies, before morphing into one of the vibiest establishments in town, with a convenient Soho location to boot. Expect thoughtful takes on everything from NYC-style pasta dishes and Mexican-influenced fare from the southwest US, to a fried chicken sandwich as a lunch special, alongside excellent cocktails and natural wines. There's also a private garden (a rarity in this part of town) that makes an ideal setting for intimate dinners and celebrations in warmer weather.

49 Lexington Street, W1F 9AP
Nearest stations: Oxford Circus, Piccadilly Circus
ritasdining.com

62

THE RITZ

The Grand Dame of London's restaurants

A symbol of London's grandeur and wealth, the restaurant at The Ritz has become – dare we say it? – sort of cool. The experience is about as opulent as you might have guessed: gawp at the decor and Rococo details as you find your way to the salon, before clocking the chandeliers and ceiling frescoes of the dining room. The food has won universal praise for the kind of elegant, familiar finesse created to delight and satisfy in equal measure. The lunch menu is a marvellous (and slightly more accessible) way to experience one of London's most special rooms, and an order of Crêpes Suzette – flambéed magnificently at your table – shows that some things never really go out of fashion.

150 Piccadilly, W1J 9BR
Nearest station: Green Park
theritzlondon.com/dine-with-us/the-ritz-restaurant

63

DONIA

Upscale Filipino cooking with swagger

Here, dynamic Filipino flavours are passed through a fine dining lens without losing any of the cuisine's essence. The lamb caldereta pie and pork lechon are stunning, and skip the ube choux pastry for dessert at your peril. While you can certainly make a dent in the menu with a friend or even flying solo, bring at least a few mates so you can order everything (and ask for extra rice to mop up the incredible sauce that each dish comes with). This is one of the most original restaurants that London has produced in a while.

2.14 Kingly Court, Carnaby Street, W1B 5PW
Nearest station: Oxford Circus
doniarestaurant.com

64

SABIIB

Somalian feasts in chic surroundings

If you haven't dug into a huge, fork-tender lamb shoulder and rice with friends, have you even done communal dining? The capital's Somalian restaurants serve up plenty of memorable experiences, and Sabiib offers a modern take without compromising on flavour or heart. Behold the slick dining room and aunties sending out platters of grilled, spiced meat accompanied by a choice of Somali spiced rice, soor (cornmeal) or pasta. Diced steak and chicken are superb, but it's hard to beat that slow-cooked lamb so soft it falls apart with a gentle prod. If you've never experienced Somalian hospitality, it's a delicious introduction – and if you have, it's a fresh way to enjoy one of London's most underrated cuisines.

139 High Street, W3 6LX
Nearest station: Acton Central
sabiibrestaurant.com

65

ESTERS

Breakfast and brunch as high art

The familiar feeling of sliding into a favourite nook at a local cafe after a brief wait plays out each weekend at Esters – except the team who run this popular no-reservations brunch spot are operating on a completely different level. Here, breakfast and brunch are placed on a pedestal and treated like high art, with spectacular results. Staples like French toast or confit pork belly with fried egg are perennial favourites, thoughtfully zhuzhed up with first-rate (and often esoteric and meticulously sourced) ingredients, like rhubarb ketchup or bee pollen-infused white chocolate. There are plenty of sophisticated and satisfying vegetarian options, and the place is usually packed.

55 Kynaston Road, N16 0EB
Nearest station: Rectory Road
estersn16.com

66

BAKE STREET

Innovative bakes and London's best smashburger

This cult cafe could be an unassuming neighbourhood coffee shop, were it not for the maniacal attention to detail and love that the owner and chefs pour into everything on the menu. Weekends see huge queues for truly ingenious pastries – the crème brûlée cookies and guava pastelitos are legendary for a reason. Meanwhile on the savoury side, fried chicken sandwiches are unimprovable, birria tacos sublime and there isn't a better smashburger in the entire city. If you've got a sweet tooth, don't miss their handmade seasonal soft serve.

58 Evering Road, N16 7SR
Nearest station: Rectory Road
instagram.com/bakestreetldn

67

OSLO COURT

Time-warp French restaurant in a housing estate

This cult French restaurant in a converted St. John's Wood housing block is so full of eccentric talking points – blushing pink decor, incredibly charming waiting staff, old-school menu of 1980s restaurant classics, plates of irresistible butter curls adorning each table – that most people forget to mention that dinner is not merely a quaint anachronism, but actually a lot of fun. A meal here, brimming with joie de vivre, is a palate cleanser in the era of small plates; a time warp to simpler pleasures. Where else are you going to find crab à la Rochelle, lobster and avocado salad and veal schnitzel Holstein, served with all the trimmings, followed by Crêpes Suzette? Exactly.

Charlbert Street, NW8 7EN
Nearest station: St. John's Wood
Phone: 020 7722 8795

68
CADET

Natural wines and renowned charcuterie

There are hip London wine bars, and then there's Cadet: an impossibly popular bolthole on Newington Green that combines every zeitgeist into a single, irresistible package – and actually pulls it off. Natural wines and friendly staff to walk you through the list? *Check*. Uncomplicatedly delicious French plates chalked up on a menu each day? *Check*. A bumping atmosphere that oozes cool, plus an in-house butcher and baker? *Check, check, check*. If you've ever been out and thought, 'I wonder if anyone else is having more fun than me?', then the answer is yes, and they're probably here.

57 Newington Green, N16 9PX
Nearest station: Canonbury
cadetlondon.com

69

BLACK AXE MANGAL

Fearlessly anarchic, Turkish-inspired menu

Black Axe Mangal has come to epitomise London's culinary creativity, and with good reason – the co-founder is a former St. John head chef, punctuating a foundation of that hearty nose-to-tail cuisine with his love of London's Turkish grills. The room is small, dark, packed and loud, beers and shots landing on tables almost as quickly as offal-laced flatbreads plucked straight from the blisteringly hot wood oven. A changing set menu could feature anything from crispy rabbit or flame-grilled lamb heart to a bone marrow and oxtail gratin or Sichuan-spiced smoked pork shoulder, plus options for vegan friends. As the owners have matured, so too has the restaurant – but thankfully, not *too* much.

156 Canonbury Road, N1 2UP
Nearest station: Highbury & Islington
blackaxemangal.com

70

TOWPATH

Chic seasonal cooking on the Haggerston riviera

Plenty of cafes have popped up along London's waterways, but this sunny establishment along the Regent's Canal differentiates itself by virtue of a laid-back Mediterranean vibe and some rather good seasonal cooking that wouldn't be out of place in the city's best kitchens. Each dish is min-imally presented and all the more stunning for it – whole roasted head of garlic on sourdough toast or a perfect smoked mackerel with pickles, say – and a semi-covered setup almost necessitates fine weather to enjoy it. You'll have to enjoy it with the rest of the neighbourhood, mind, as it's very popu-lar – but getting there early is well worth the effort.

42 De Beauvoir Crescent, N1 5SB
Nearest station: Haggerston
towpathlondon.com

71
QUINCE

A very British bakery from a very fine dining chef

What if I saved you the last brown butter bun? European styles dominate London's top bakeries, which is part of what makes this Islington spot so special. Here, there's a return to British tradition, and at the helm, one of the country's most talented bakers and a former fine dining pastry chef. Its signature buns are covetable, and despite the neighbourhood feel, Quince inevitably draws a crowd who come for perfect country loaves, tatty scones, Guinness bread still warm from the oven and excellent fruit pies and tarts. Grab an Allpress coffee or a cup of guest filter and join the queue.

267 New North Road, N1 7AA
Nearest station: Essex Road
quincebakery.co.uk

72

THE PLIMSOLL

Pints, nostalgia and an all-conquering cheeseburger

Most chefs – even the ones that wear tall white hats and stage at restaurants in Copenhagen with unpronounceable names – want to be publicans deep down, and the owners of this Finsbury Park boozer put in time at some of London and Paris's finest hotspots before crowdfunding their way to that dream with The Plimsoll. Locals visit for a drink and the football, but no one will judge you for dining here – especially when the food's this good. The menu is a mixture of French bistronomy and playful British fare – pigeon bhuna, pâté-en-croûte, chicken cooked in vin jaune – but every order needs to include at least one Dexter beef cheeseburger, a strong contender for the best in the city.

52 St Thomas's Road, N4 2QQ
Nearest station: Finsbury Park
instagram.com/the.plimsoll

73

NECO TANTUNI

Hyper-specialised Turkish dishes

This unassuming neighbourhood cafe in Enfield focuses on a holy trinity of dishes. As the name suggests, the primary offering is tantuni – the famed late-night Turkish snack of seasoned diced lamb, balanced with tomatoes and rolled in thin lavash bread like a perfect meat cigar. The yogurtlu tantuni (here, doused with yoghurt and brown butter) is superb and buys you time to contemplate a second, third or fourth order. But arguably the standout offering is the kunefe, a crisp, sticky Palestinian dessert of spun pastry soaked in attar (syrup) and layered with cheese. The owners hail from the dish's hometown, and their expertise and dedication shines through.

4 Brick Lane, Enfield, EN3 5BA
Nearest station: Southbury
instagram.com/neco_tantuni_ve_kunefe

74

SAMBAL SHIOK LAKSA BAR

Flawless laksas and feel-good Malaysian snacks

The labour that goes into a single bowl of noodles can be breathtaking, and few bowls exemplify this quite like the painstakingly crafted Malaysian laksa at this popular Highbury hotspot. Owner Mandy Yin's Kuala Lumpur upbringing comes across in the spicy coconut broth of her signature dish, which arrives at your table loaded with egg noodles, chicken or plump prawns and tofu puffs to soak up all that gorgeous liquid. It's a perfect meal as is, but don't overlook the sweet service, the sides (the fried chicken is legendary) and specials, like a hot and sour assam laksa. Come patio season, relaxing after dinner with a pandan spritz is a particular pleasure.

171 Holloway Road, N7 8LX
Nearest stations: Highbury & Islington, Drayton Park
sambalshiok.co.uk

75

TRULLO

Radiant Italian cooking

The neighbourhood Italian is a beloved standby across the city, but few feel quite as special as this gem in Highbury. It's deliberately unshowy, but markers of quality are everywhere, from the pressed linens adorning each table and the rigorously trained staff who wear their knowledge lightly, to the understated, seasonal dishes that shine with the finest produce and ineffable skill. Pastas and desserts here are famous, but equally spellbinding is the atmosphere, low lighting, red wine and thrum of a dozen sparkling conversations. You'll want to return as soon as you leave.

300–302 St Paul's Road, N1 2LH
Nearest station: Highbury & Islington
trullorestaurant.com

76

SONORA TAQUERÍA

London's best tacos, full-stop

This adored Stoke Newington taquería began to draw massive queues shortly after it was founded. Co-founder Michelle Salazar de la Rocha hails from Mexico's northern state of Sonora, where wheat tacos are king. She hand presses and layers these with impeccable carne asada (grilled beef) or tender nopales (cactus), as well as flavoursome braises like barbacoa (slow-cooked beef) or fork-tender ox tongue and cheek. The menu is short but sweet, and you'll be wanting for little else: even on repeat visits, something this perfect can never get old.

77

PEPPERS & SPICE

Beatified Caribbean takeaway adored by locals

Cut London open and you'll find it bleeds ackee and saltfish. A cornerstone of London's diaspora food culture, a good Caribbean takeaway satisfies and nourishes like nothing else, and this popular Dalston spot is a beacon for anyone craving saltfish patties, oxtail, curry goat and a side of macaroni or rice and peas. Their jerk chicken is marinated before being cooked in the oven and finished on the grill; biting into the spiced, burnished skin and succulent meat is a rite of passage for many Londoners. The short list of specials changes each day, and it gets busy around dinnertime, so expect to queue.

40 Balls Pond Road, N1 4AU
Nearest station: Dalston Junction
Other location: Tottenham
peppersandspicetakeaway.co.uk

IMAGE CREDITS

Page 2 © Ola Smit; page 4-5 © Harriet Langford; page 6 © David Post; page 7 © Sam A. Harris; page 8 © Paola Vivas; page 9 © Alexander Baxter; Luca first image © Anton Rodriguez, second image © Joe Woodhouse; Master Wei Xi'an © David Post; Otto's © David Post; Parsons © Barnaby Newton; St. John first two images © Sam A. Harris, third image © Stefan Johnson; The Clove Club © Helen Cathcart; Sessions Arts Club © Louise Long; The Quality Chop House all images © Sam A. Harris; Noble Rot first image © Tom Cockram, second image © Juan Trujillo Andrades; The Eagle Farringdon © David Post; Bánh Mì Hội-An © David Post; Beigel Bake © Charlotte Schreiber; Mangal 1 © David Post; Afghan Grill © Martin Usborne; Brawn © Helen Cathcart; Andu Cafe © Helen Cathcart; Ananthapuram all images © David Post; Facing Heaven © Sam A. Harris; E. Pellicci © Rachael Smith; Bistrotheque first image © Helen Cathcart, following images © Anton Rodriguez; Etles © David Post; Mambow © Marcus Spooner; Pockets © David Post; E5 Bakehouse © Sam A. Harris; Morito © Helen Cathcart; Planque © Anton Rodriguez; Polentina all images © David Post; Sushi Show © David Post; Café Cecilia all images © Maureen M Evans (http://www.maureenme.com); Lyle's all images © Anton Rodriguez; Pophams all images © Adrianna Giakoumis; Rochelle Canteen © Helen Cathcart; Singburi © Elliot Roston; Eat Vietnam © David Post; Imone © Hazel Fung @hay_lets_eat; Kaieteur Kitchen © David Post; Bravi Ragazzi © Bravi Ragazzi; Eric's © Milly Kenny-Ryder; BAO Borough all images © Marcus Cobden; Rambutan © Matt Russell; 40 Maltby Street © Trent McMinn; Kapihan © Matthew Hickman, image courtesy Kapihan; Berenjak all images © Marcus Cobden; Akub all images © Matthew Hague; Crisp Pizza W6 © Tom Cockram; Café TPT all images © David Post; Barrafina © Alexander Baxter; Dorian all images © Lesley Lau; Gymkhana first and third images © Marcus Cobden, second image © Mark Scott; Hunan © Featherston Haugh Photography; Chishuru © Harriet Langford; Darjeeling Express all images © Ming Tang Evans / @mintangevans; Endo at the Rotunda all images © Food Story Media; Koya © Per-Anders Jorgensen; The Palomar © Ariana Ruth; Quo Vadis all images © Alexander Baxter; Mountain © Benjamin McMahon; The Harwood Arms all images © Orlando Gili; Andrew Edmunds © Nick Moore / Alamy Stock Photo; Paul Rothe & Son all images © Rachael Smith; Rita's © Paola Vivas; The Ritz © The Ritz London / John Carey; Donia © Karl King Aguña; Sabiib © Sabiib Somali Restaurant; Esters © David Post; Bake Street © David Post; Oslo Court all images © David Post; Cadet © Sam A. Harris; Black Axe Mangal © Ola Smit; Towpath all images © Helen Cathcart; Quince Bakery © Milly Kenny-Ryder; The Plimsoll all images © David Post; Neco Tantuni © Nick Bramham; Sambal Shiok Laksa Bar first image © Mandy Yin, second image © Chris Keeling, third image © Kar Shing Tong; Trullo © Trullo; Sonora Taqueria © David Post; Peppers & Spice © David Post.

*An Opinionated Guide
to London Food*
First edition, second printing

Published in 2024
by Hoxton Mini Press, London

Copyright © Hoxton Mini Press 2024.
All rights reserved.

Text by David Paw
Editing by Florence Ward
Design and production
by Richard Mason
Proofreading by Zoë Jellicoe
Editorial support by Leona Crawford

With thanks to Matthew Young for
initial series design.

Please note: we recommend checking
the websites listed for each entry
before you visit for the latest
information on price, opening times
and pre-booking requirements.

A CIP catalogue record for this book
is available from the British Library.

ISBN: 978-1-914314-65-0

Printed and bound by OZGraf, Poland

Hoxton Mini Press is an environmen-
tally conscious publisher, committed
to offsetting our carbon footprint.
This book is 100 per cent carbon
compensated, with offset purchased
from Stand For Trees.

Every time you order from
our website, we plant a tree:
www.hoxtonminipress.com

MIX
Paper | Supporting
responsible forestry
FSC® C163799
FSC
www.fsc.org

Selected opinionated guides in the series:

For more go to www.hoxtonminipress.com

INDEX